Toothoak's Tooth Fairies

Written by
Jose Alvarez DDS

Illustrated by
Marvin Alonso

Toothhoak's Tooth Fairies

ISBN: 978-1-7334982-1-0

Written by: Jose Alvarez DDS

Editing by: Delgar Publishing
Cover and Interior design: Marvin Alonso

This book is dedicated to

My beautiful family. Love you with all my heart.

Once upon a time in a magical forest far far away live the tooth fairies.

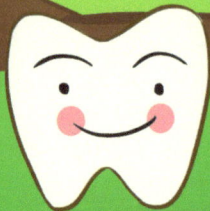

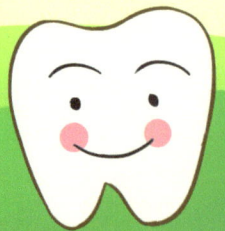

There is a very special tree here. It's called the Tooth Oak Tree.

When a tooth fairy buries a kid's tooth in the ground, the tree grows big and strong. The tree grows money for the kids and provides air to the tooth fairies to breath.

But there is a Problem in the forest, the evil witch loves making brooms sticks from trees in the forest.

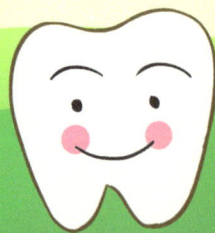

Fortunately, tooth oak trees are witch proof and she can't cut down tooth oak trees for broom sticks.

Hooray, no more broomsticks for the sad witch!!

So help the fairies plant more tooth oak trees. When you go to bed, put your tooth under your pillow and say "Fairy, Fairy take my tooth, I will be sleeping and that's the truth. If you plant my tooth with glee, I promise it will grow to be a beautiful tooth oak tree."

So just remember, by leaving your tooth for the tooth fairies tonight, you will be helping them stay happy and healthy.

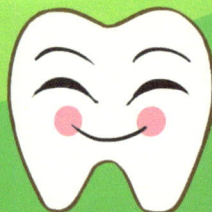

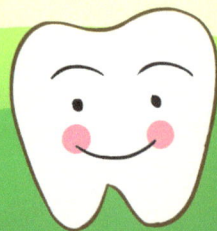

Now don't forget the magic words. Have a good night kiddo. Thanks for helping us out!

The End

www.ingramcontent.com/pod-product-compliance
Lightning Source LLC
Chambersburg PA
CBHW042020090426

42811CB00015B/1694